Series 536

CONTENTS

A LADYBIRD BOOK

YOUR
BODY

by DAVID SCOTT DANIELL
with illustrations by ROBERT AYTON

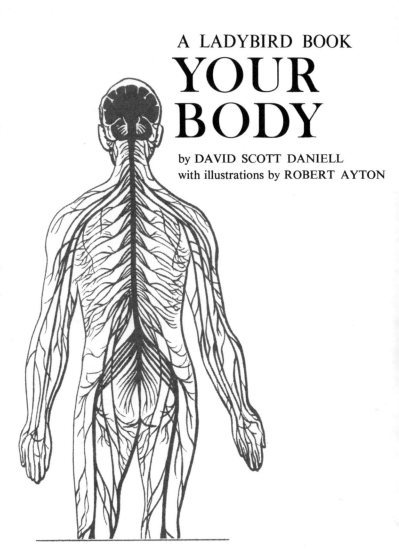

Publishers WILLS & HEPWORTH Ltd Loughborough
First published 1967   ©   *Printed in England*

Your Skeleton

Your body is constructed on a framework of bones, the skeleton. Like every part of your body, the skeleton is wonderfully designed for its purpose. It gives your body shape, protects all the soft and sensitive parts inside, and has a number of joints so that you can move. The main parts are the skull, the trunk and the limbs.

The skull is made of twenty-two separate bones joined together to make a strong case for your brain, eyes, ears, nose and mouth. The only part of the skull which can be moved is the lower jaw, which is hinged so that you can open your mouth.

The trunk consists of the spinal column, or back-bone, the breast-bone, the ribs and the pelvis. The spinal column has thirty-three knobbly bones called *vertebrae*, separated by discs of gristle—cartilage—rather like washers between metal parts in a machine. These make it possible to move the back-bone, and serve as shock-absorbers to protect the delicate vertebrae from shock. The vertebrae at the lower end of the spine are called the *coccyx*, and this is all that remains of the tail once possessed by man.

Twelve pairs of ribs are connected to your back-bone, ten of them curving round to join the breast-bone. Ribs and breast-bone form your chest, which protects your heart and lungs.

4

7214 0108 2

BACK VIEW OF SKELETON

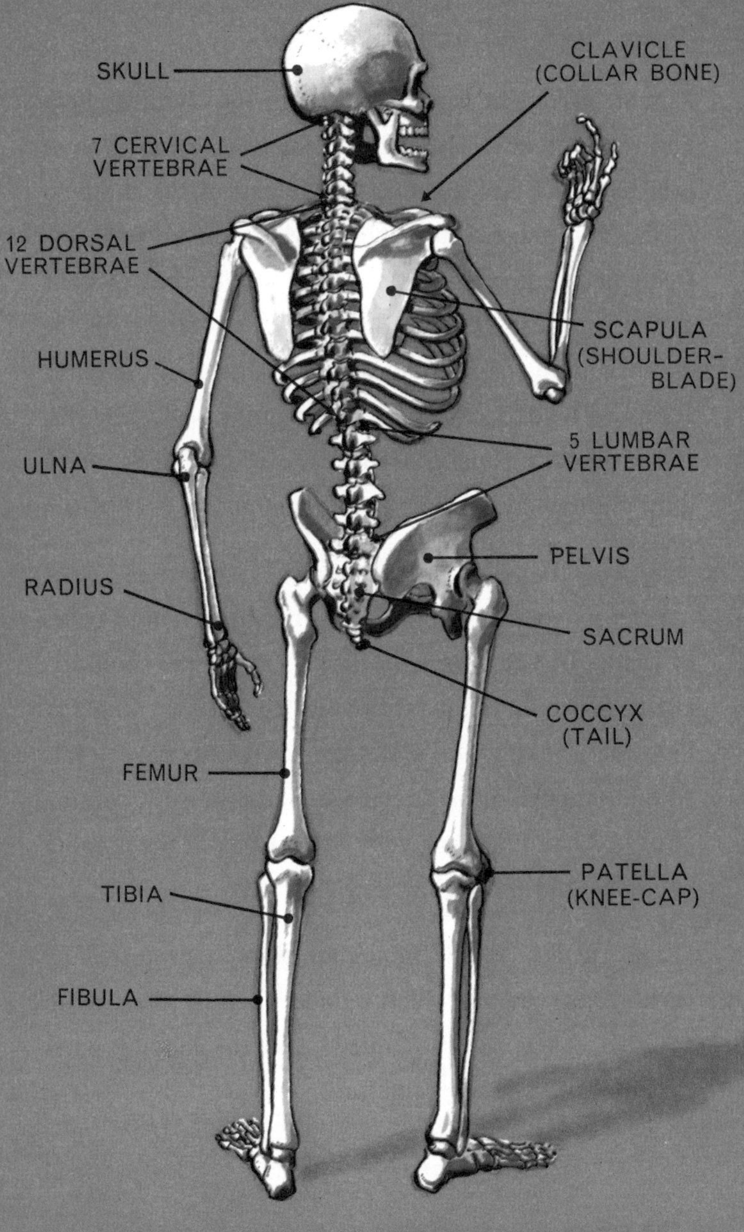

SKULL

CLAVICLE
(COLLAR BONE)

7 CERVICAL
VERTEBRAE

12 DORSAL
VERTEBRAE

SCAPULA
(SHOULDER-
BLADE)

HUMERUS

5 LUMBAR
VERTEBRAE

ULNA

PELVIS

RADIUS

SACRUM

COCCYX
(TAIL)

FEMUR

PATELLA
(KNEE-CAP)

TIBIA

FIBULA

Your Skeleton at Work

Your arms and legs are joined to the trunk by ball-and-socket joints. The ball of bone at the top of your arm-bone fits into a socket at the end of the shoulder blade. This makes it possible for you to move your arm freely in any direction. In the same way the ball of bone at the top of your thigh fits into a deep socket in the *pelvis*, a basin-shaped bone at the lower end of the spine. Joints are held together by strong bands called *ligaments*. Other joints, such as your ankles, are like hinges, which only permit movement in a general up and down direction.

Free movement is made possible by a whole series of joints. In your arm you have joints at the shoulder, elbow, wrist, and fingers; in your leg there are joints at hip, knee, ankle, foot and toes. You also have joints so that you can move your head, and others for turning your body and bending your back. Look at the number of joints used in bowling a cricket ball.

The surface on the bones at joints is protected by cartilage, or gristle, which reduces friction as they rub together. They are also ' oiled ', like the moving parts of a machine, by a special fluid.

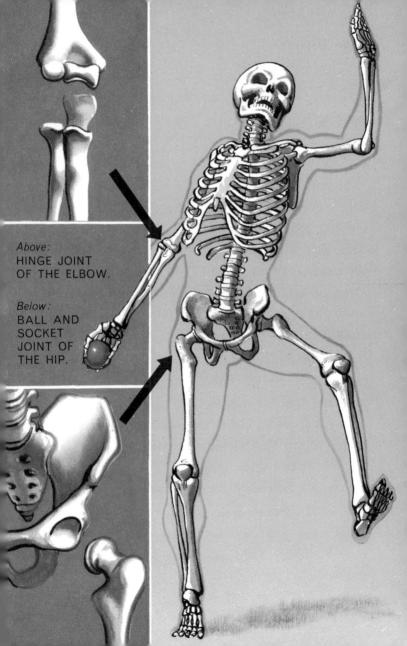

Above:
HINGE JOINT
OF THE ELBOW.

Below:
BALL AND
SOCKET
JOINT OF
THE HIP.

The Muscles

Every joint in your body is controlled by *muscles*, which are bundles of fibres forming the flesh. Muscles are usually in the shape of long, thin cells called fibres. They are fastened to the joints by strong cords of fibrous tissue, called *tendons*.

Muscles are arranged in layers, one on top of the other, intricately and wonderfully positioned to give efficient control to every moving part of the body. Movement is brought about by contracting or relaxing the muscles. When you bend your elbow you can feel the hard lump of contracted muscle called the biceps, under the skin. The muscles give strength to the limbs, and the stronger your muscles, the stronger you are.

Every time you bend your arm or move your wrist or fingers, you use the muscles in your arm. You use muscles when you walk or run, turn your head, bend down, or make any movement. The muscles in your face enable you to change your expression; to laugh, grin, cry, blink or twitch your nose. Your strong jaw muscles are used when you eat or talk.

Some muscles operate without you knowing, as much when you are asleep as awake. These control your breathing, digestion, the working of your heart and so on.

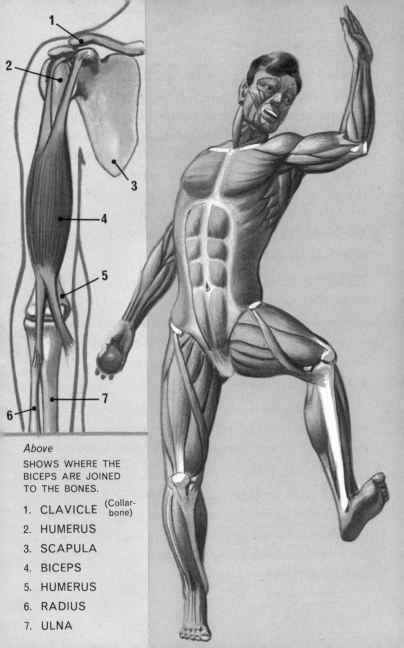

Above

SHOWS WHERE THE
BICEPS ARE JOINED
TO THE BONES.

1. CLAVICLE (Collar-bone)

2. HUMERUS

3. SCAPULA

4. BICEPS

5. HUMERUS

6. RADIUS

7. ULNA

Your Skin

In scientific language we can say that the skin is the largest organ of the body. It is a perfectly fitting waterproof container for all the varied and complicated parts of your body. Its thickness varies; it is very thin on your eyelids, thick on your back and very thick on the palms of your hands and soles of your feet. You have two skins, each consisting of several layers. The outer skin is the *epidermis*, and the inner skin is the *dermis*. The dermis contains a fine network of blood-vessels, nerves, sweat glands and hair roots.

The skin helps to regulate the temperature of your body. When you are hot, tiny pores open and let out, or *excrete*, sweat, and as this evaporates in the air your skin is cooled. This excretion of sweat and waste matter through the pores of the skin is the reason you must wash to keep it clean.

When you are cold the skin gets what we call ' goose-flesh ', which is caused by tiny muscles in the skin making the hairs stand up to provide warmth, as an animal's fur fluffs up in the cold.

Hairs grow through your skin all over your body, except on the palms of your hands and soles of your feet. Length and thickness varies; it is long and close on your head, thick and close in your eyebrows and short and sparse elsewhere.

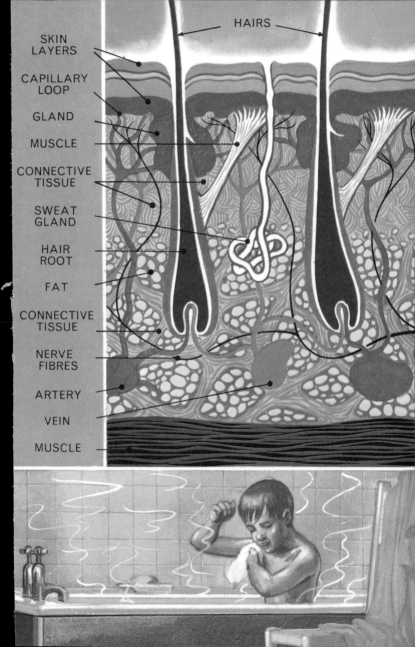

HAIRS

SKIN LAYERS

CAPILLARY LOOP

GLAND

MUSCLE

CONNECTIVE TISSUE

SWEAT GLAND

HAIR ROOT

FAT

CONNECTIVE TISSUE

NERVE FIBRES

ARTERY

VEIN

MUSCLE

Your Central Nervous System

The central nervous system of your body consists of the brain and the spinal cord. The brain is a complicated mass of grey and white matter contained in three layers of tissue, called *meninges*. It is protected by the strong bone casing of the skull. The brain is a large organ; a grown man's weighs more than three pounds and it is not much less in a child of seven. With your brain you think, remember, feel, and control the movements of your body.

The brain has two main divisions, the *cerebrum* in the front upper part of the skull and the *cerebellum* in the back lower part. These are divided into a right and left half by a deep groove. The surface of the cerebrum forms folds and ridges.

The spinal cord is an extension of the brain which continues down inside the spinal canal, in the centre of the spinal column. For the last third of the way it tapers off into a slender thread, which joins the coccyx at the base of the spine.

Pearly white nerves branch off in pairs from each side of the spinal cord between the vertibrae. These nerves extend into every part of the body, as is explained in the next page. Through the spinal cord the nerves are connected with the ' headquarters ' of the body, the brain.

1. THOUGHT
2. ELABORATION OF CONSCIOUS
3. SWALLOWING
4. MASTICATION
5. TONGUE CONTROL
6. FACE CONTROL
7. HAND CONTROL
8. ARM CONTROL
9. BODY CONTROL
10. LEG CONTROL
11. HEARING
12. SPEECH
13. VISUAL & AUDITORY RECOLLECTION
14. PERCEPTUAL JUDGEMENT
15. VISION

CEREBRUM

CEREBELLUM

SPINAL CORD

Your Nerves

Your nerves are a complicated organisation of links between different parts of your body and your brain. It is as if you had a network of telephone lines by which signals are passed to and from the brain. Nerves are delicate, white threads of varying thickness, usually dividing again and again to spread like the branches of a tree.

Nerves do different kinds of jobs. One set, the *special senses*, comes directly from the lower part of the brain, and is concerned with seeing, hearing, smelling and tasting. The *sensory nerves* inform the brain about feel, heat and pain. These go from the spinal cord, reaching to every part of your body. Pick up something and close your eyes. The nerves in your hand and fingers tell your brain a great deal of information about what you hold, its shape, size, temperature—the nerves describe it.

The name *motor nerves* tells you what these nerves do; they control movement by taking orders from your brain to your muscles.

If you touch something very hot you snatch your hand away, or if something comes dangerously near your eyes you close them. This is done 'without thinking', and is called *reflex action*. (*See pages 48 and 49*)

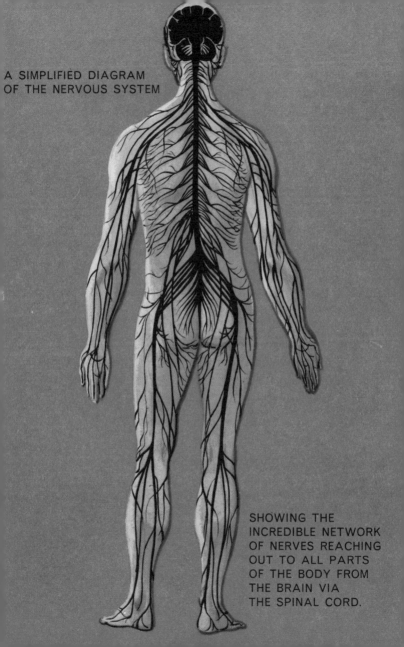

A SIMPLIFIED DIAGRAM
OF THE NERVOUS SYSTEM

SHOWING THE
INCREDIBLE NETWORK
OF NERVES REACHING
OUT TO ALL PARTS
OF THE BODY FROM
THE BRAIN VIA
THE SPINAL CORD.

Your Motor and Autonomic Nerves

When you want to move any part of your body, your brain sends an order down the *motor* nerves, which connect with the muscles which operate the joints. Every movement you wish to make is ordered by your brain; whether it be to turn your neck, move any of your limbs, open your mouth or twitch your nose. If you decide to move a chair towards you and sit down, your brain sends a series of messages down the appropriate motor nerves to your shoulders, elbows, hands and fingers to move the chair, and to your knees, feet, back and other limbs to sit down. These messages are passed so quickly that it all seems instantaneous.

Not all movement is controlled by the brain, some occurs by the operation of another nervous system, the self-governing or *autonomic* nerves. These control the many movements of the body necessary to life. They operate your breathing, keep your heart pumping and change the rate when necessary, control digestion and a score of other processes such as the movement of the intestines, all without you realising what is happening.

When you are asleep your body continues to function. You breathe, your blood flows through arteries and veins and heart, your digestive organs work, and the body provides the moisture necessary for your eyes, mouth and throat.

THE AUTONOMIC NERVES KEEP YOU ALIVE AS YOU SLEEP

THE HEART CONTINUES TO PUMP.

THE LUNGS PROVIDE OXYGEN.

THE DIGESTIVE ORGANS CONTINUE
WITH THEIR SORTING-OUT PROCESS.

THE BODY TEMPERATURE IS
KEPT EVEN.

MOISTURE IS PROVIDED FOR
THE EYES, NOSE, MOUTH
AND THROAT.

The Cells of your Body

Your body is made up of countless millions of living cells. Each cell consists of a *nucleus*, floating in *protoplasm* contained within a *membrane*. The nucleus is the headquarters of a cell; it gives it its character and directs its work. Protoplasm is a colourless jelly and the membrane is an exceedingly thin, porous skin, through which oxygen and food pass into the cell and waste passes out.

There are many different kinds of cell, which may be grouped into four classes. The *epithelial* cells are in layers forming the skin and the inside surfaces of internal organs. The cells of the *connective tissue* bind and hold everything together and form gristle and tendons. *Bone and cartilage* cells make up the skeleton. *Muscular* cells are bundles of fibres which enable you to move your joints. *Nerve* cells, long and slender, connect every part of the body with the brain.

Every cell has a special job; for example, those in the pancreas make insulin which controls the level of sugar in the blood. Cells die, but they produce new cells of the same kind. Cells of the skin are renewed in less than a week, others live for many months. The exception is the nerve cell which is never renewed.

SOME HUMAN CELLS

SKIN

NERVE

MUSCLE

BONE

GLAND

CONNECTIVE TISSUE

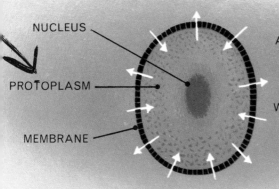

NUCLEUS

PROTOPLASM

MEMBRANE

ARROWS DENOTE
ABSORPTION OF
NUTRIMENT AND
EXCRETION OF
WASTE THROUGH
THE POROUS
MEMBRANE.

The Circulation of the Blood

The heart works like a pump, beating eighty times a minute and sending the blood circulating through your body. When the doctor feels your pulse he is feeling the artery at your wrist and counting the rate of your heart beat. In the heart there are four chambers, or cavities, called the *right auricle*, *right ventricle*, *left auricle* and *left ventricle*. The blood is circulated through *arteries*, *veins* and *capillaries*. Let us follow the blood on its long journey through your body.

Bright red blood is pumped *from* the left ventricle of your heart into the main artery (*aorta*). From this, other arteries lead off, getting smaller and smaller as they reach into every part of your body, until they become microscopically small capillaries. These have very thin walls through which oxygen and food pass into the minute cells of the body-tissues. The capillaries also take waste material from the tissues, so that blood both feeds and cleans.

The impure blood, dark red in colour, shown as blue in the diagram, passes from the capillaries into the veins, which take it back *to* the heart. It enters the right auricle and passes to the right ventricle.

Then it begins a second circuit, through the *pulmonary* system. It is pumped through the pulmonary arteries to the lungs. Here the used oxygen, carbon dioxide, is removed, new oxygen is added, and the pulmonary veins take the refreshed blood, now bright red again, back to the left auricle, and so into the left ventricle, to start the circulation again.

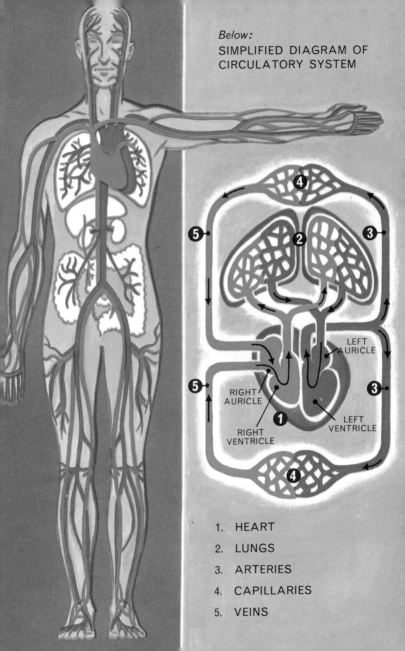

Below:
SIMPLIFIED DIAGRAM OF
CIRCULATORY SYSTEM

LEFT
AURICLE

RIGHT
AURICLE

RIGHT
VENTRICLE

LEFT
VENTRICLE

1. HEART
2. LUNGS
3. ARTERIES
4. CAPILLARIES
5. VEINS

Your Blood

Blood is composed of *plasma*, red and white *blood corpuscles* (or cells), and *platelets*. As we read in the last page, blood carries nourishment and oxygen to the tissues of the body, and carries away the waste.

Plasma is a straw-coloured fluid which supports the blood corpuscles and platelets. The blood corpuscles are so small that about five million of the red corpuscles are contained in a cubic millimetre of blood.

The plasma carries nourishment which has been extracted from your food and drink, and then collects waste material and delivers it to the kidneys, to be excreted from the body.

The red corpuscles carry oxygen from the lungs, after you have breathed it in, and take it round to all your tissues. They, too, collect waste, by taking the used oxygen, called carbon dioxide, and delivering it to the lungs to be breathed out.

The white blood corpuscles are health protectors, for they destroy disease organisms in your blood. You have one white blood corpuscle for about five hundred red.

The platelets, which are smaller even than the blood corpuscles, cause blood to congeal, and so stop bleeding from a small cut by forming a clot to seal it.

Sometimes when people are ill, or have lost a lot of blood, they need a 'blood transfusion'. Volunteers, like the one in the picture, give blood which is stored in special containers ready for an emergency.

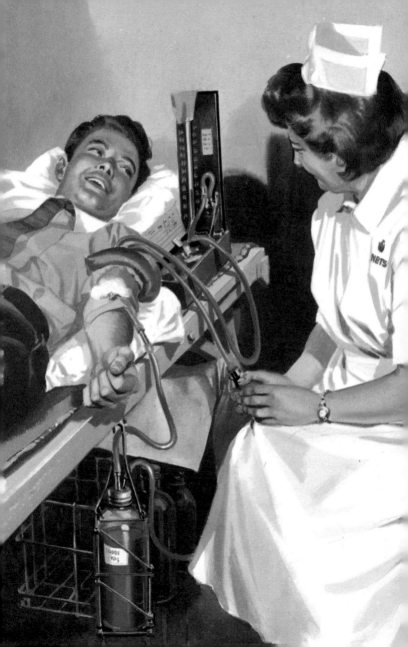

How you Breathe

Your lungs work like a pair of bellows. They are in your chest behind the ribs, and beneath them is an arched muscle, the diaphragm. You open the bellows to breathe in by raising your ribs and pressing down the diaphragm. This makes your chest larger, lowers the pressure in your lungs, and so air goes in, through your nose or mouth. When you close the bellows, your ribs return to the normal position, the diaphragm rises, the lungs are squeezed, and so you breathe out.

Normally you breathe about sixteen times a minute, but when you need more air, as when you are running, you breathe faster, and the bellows work harder. You can see your chest rising and falling.

When you breathe in, the air passes into your windpipe, or *trachea*, which divides into two tubes called the *bronchi* which pass into your pair of lungs. The bronchi divide and branch until they are a mass of very tiny tubes ending in *air-sacs*. The oxygen is able to pass through the thin walls of the air-sacs into the blood vessels in the lungs, and so into the blood stream, and the oxygen needed by your tissues flows all over your body. The used oxygen, *carbon dioxide*, passes from the blood vessels into the air-vessels, and so up the bronchi to the windpipe to be breathed out.

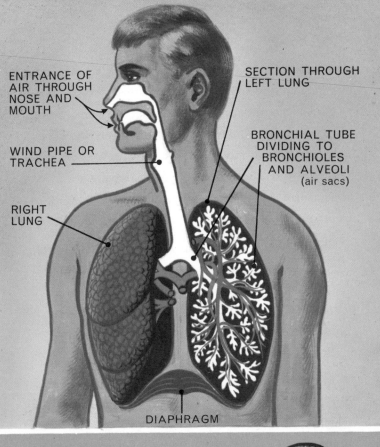

ENTRANCE OF
AIR THROUGH
NOSE AND
MOUTH

SECTION THROUGH
LEFT LUNG

WIND PIPE OR
TRACHEA

BRONCHIAL TUBE
DIVIDING TO
BRONCHIOLES
AND ALVEOLI
(air sacs)

RIGHT
LUNG

DIAPHRAGM

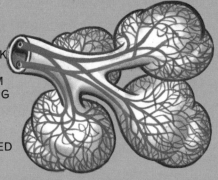

GREATLY MAGNIFIED
PORTION OF ALVEOLI
OR AIR CAVITIES.
SHOWING THE NETWORK
OF CAPILLARY VEINS
CARRYING BLOOD FROM
THE HEART, EXTRACTING
OXYGEN THROUGH THE
THIN MEMBRANE OF
THE AIR BAGS AND
CONVEYING OXYGENATED
BLOOD BACK INTO THE
BLOOD STREAM.

What happens to your Food

Before your food can be absorbed into your blood it has to be changed considerably, and this process is called *digestion*. You first cut up your food into small pieces with your teeth, while a fluid called *saliva* reduces it to a soft pulp in your mouth, stirred by your tongue. When it is ready to be swallowed it passes down a soft, fleshy tube, called the *oesophagus*, which goes down in front of your spinal column to your stomach.

The pulp is again stirred up, this time by the movement of the stomach muscles, and it is acted on by the *gastric juices* inside the stomach to continue preparation for absorption by the blood. Some of the liquids in the pulp are absorbed through the walls of the stomach during this process and pass into the blood.

After from two to six hours the remaining food passes into the *small intestine*, a tube some twenty feet long which is wonderfully folded and packed. Here more fluids, coming from the liver and the *pancreas* continue the digestive process, extracting the good from the food and passing it into your blood. Finally the indigestible matter goes into the large intestine, moving slowly into the lower part, the rectum, (sometimes referred to as the bowels), until it is later expelled from the body through the anus.

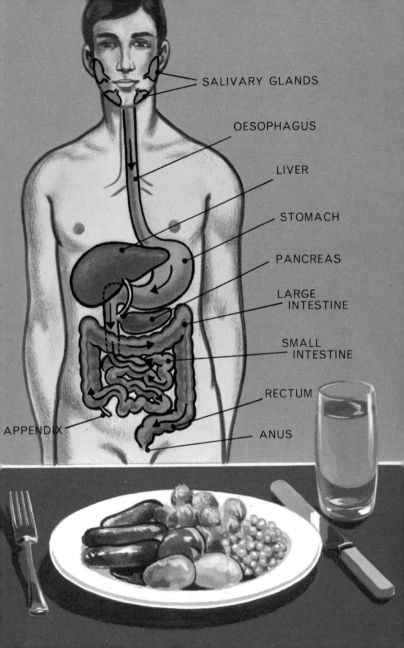

SALIVARY GLANDS

OESOPHAGUS

LIVER

STOMACH

PANCREAS

LARGE INTESTINE

SMALL INTESTINE

RECTUM

APPENDIX

ANUS

Your Liver and Kidneys

The liver is a large reddish-brown organ, under the right side of your diaphragm, and has an important duty in the process of digestion. It makes *bile*, one of the digestive juices, and it also changes the food absorbed from the intestines, converting it into substances suitable for absorption by the body cells. It stores any excess for future use. Protein which is not required is broken down into *urea* and passed to the kidneys to be excreted from the body as *urine*.

You have two kidneys, one on each side of your spinal column at the back. Some of the blood from the aorta passes to the kidneys to be filtered. The big corpuscles and other valuable cells cannot pass out, but waste-matter can and passes as a yellowish liquid, called urine, down two tubes called ureter to be stored in the bladder. Later it is passed out of the body via the urethra.

All waste-matter has to be removed. Carbon dioxide is breathed out from the lungs through the nose and mouth. Impurities in the skin are excreted through the sweat glands. Solid waste is excreted from the bowels, at the lower end of the large intestine, via the anus. Liquid is excreted as urine.

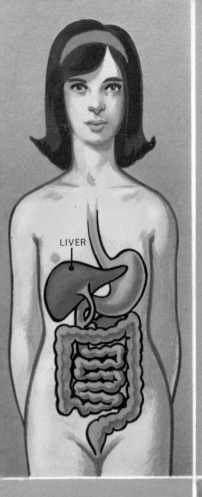

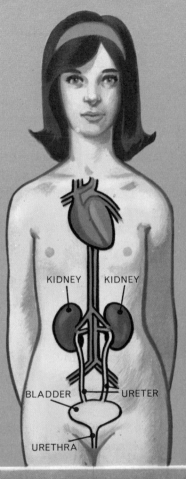

SECRETIONS FROM THE
LIVER HELP TO BREAK
DOWN SOLID FOOD INTO
THE LIQUIDS THAT THE
BODY CELLS CAN USE.
WASTE MATTER IS
EXCRETED.

BLOOD PASSES TO THE
KIDNEYS TO BE FILTERED.
WASTE MATTER FROM THE
BLOOD, AND EXCESS LIQUID
PASS FROM THE BODY AS
URINE VIA THE BLADDER,

Stoking up the Body

A stoker shovels coal into the firebox of an engine. It burns and generates heat and energy to drive the engine. You take food in at your mouth, and that, too, is 'burned' to generate heat and energy for the body. Food is the body's fuel, and it is 'burned' in the body-cells with the oxygen from the blood. The 'smoke' is the carbon dioxide you breathe out. Food consists of three main substances; *carbohydrates, proteins* and *fats*.

Carbohydrates are found in bread, pastry and cakes, potatoes and other starchy vegetables, in sugar, fruit and milk. Proteins are in meat, fish, eggs, milk and cheese. When your food is split up during digestion the proteins are taken by the blood to repair worn tissues and to make the new ones in young growing people. Fats come from meat, milk, butter and some vegetables. They are vital to the nourishment of the body and when not required at once they are stored, notably by 'fat' people.

In addition to the main foods, you must have *vitamins*. There are five main ones, A, B, C, D and E, and they all perform necessary functions for health and growth. Vitamins are contained in animal fats, eggs, milk and particularly in fresh fruit, fresh vegetables and cereals. You must also have plenty of water and certain salts. For good health and growth you must eat a balanced diet of all the foods the body needs.

CARBOHYDRATES

PROTEINS

FATS

Your Body's Cooling System

The body-cells burn food with oxygen and generate heat, and when you are more active than usual more food is burned and more heat is generated. Yet in summer and winter, whether you are sitting still or running about, the temperature of your body is about the same, roughly between 98°F and 99°F, with the normal temperature in the mouth 98.4°F. (36.9°C.)

Your body has a number of ways of cooling itself to maintain a normal temperature. When you are hot you breathe faster, or pant, and so lose heat from the body in the breath. On a cold day you can see your breath as the hot moisture in it condenses. When you exert yourself, your heart beats faster to pump more blood round your body, particularly to the skin, where the sweat-glands open and the sweat evaporates and so cools you. Since you lose more fluid from the body when you are hot, you become thirsty and want to pour more liquid in.

As the extra blood flows near the surface of the skin it is cooled, and so cools the whole body. It is the same principle as cooling the hot water in a car engine through the radiator. So much blood is pumped from the heart when you run hard that it gushes into the arteries like water from a tap. When you are hot your instinct is to keep still, when you are cold you want to move about.

How you See

The eye is such a delicate organ that it is particularly well protected. It is set in a strong, bone eye-socket in the skull, well lined with soft fat. Eye lids protect the front, with lashes to keep out dust, eye brows to keep out sweat and rain, and a supply of a liquid, tears, to keep the round eye-ball washed clean.

The eye is protected at the front by a transparent layer called the *cornea*. Looking at the eye from the front, the coloured part is the *iris*, and the black circle is the *pupil*. This is a hole into the interior of the eye-ball, and looks black because the interior of the eye-ball is dark. The pupil widens or closes according to the amount of light falling on the eye ; it is widest at night and smallest in bright light.

Behind the iris is suspended the *lens* through which the rays of light pass on to the *retina*, which is the light-sensitive inner layer shown in the diagram. On the retina, the rays of light form a small image (upside down) of what you see, and this is passed along the *optic nerve* to the brain where it is turned the right way up. In the same way, a camera lens inverts an image on to a film. Your eye collects the message, your brain interprets it — and you see.

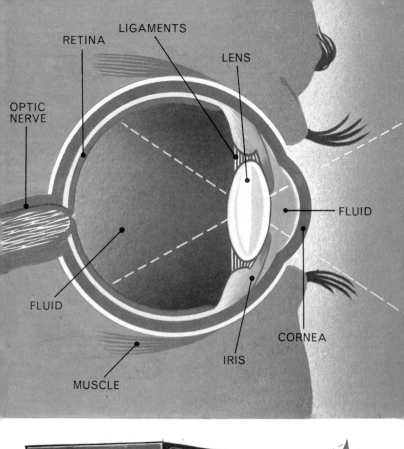

RETINA

LIGAMENTS

LENS

OPTIC NERVE

FLUID

FLUID

CORNEA

IRIS

MUSCLE

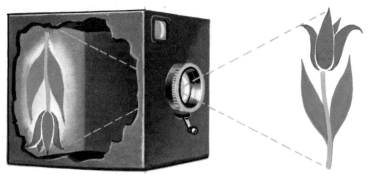

How you Hear

The ear you see is a fleshy, shell-shaped organ to catch sound-waves and reflect them into what is called the *auditory canal*. This secretes ear-wax, and is separated from the middle ear by a tightly stretched piece of skin called the *ear-drum*. The middle ear is a semi-bony tube, separated from the inner ear by a membrane.

When sound waves are collected by the outer ear they make the ear-drum vibrate. These vibrations are carried to the inner ear by a system of small, delicate bones linked together, called the hammer, the anvil and the stirrup. The inner ear is filled with liquid through which the vibrations are transmitted via nerves to the brain.

The other part of the inner ear is concerned with balance, and consists of three semi-circular canals or tubes in the form of loops. Any movement of the liquid inside them warns your brain and so enables you to maintain your balance. It is like a very clever kind of spirit level. When you spin round, the balancing system is confused, and you feel dizzy and tend to fall over.

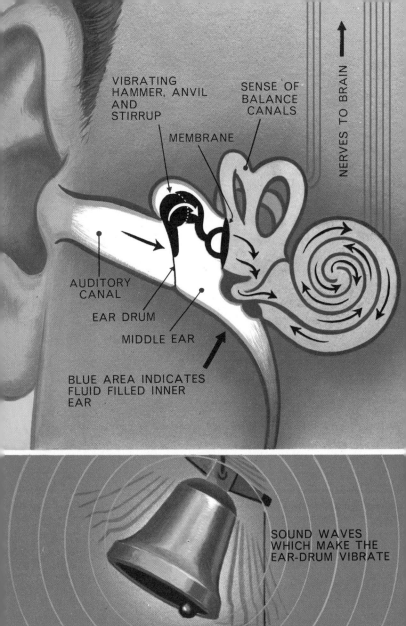

VIBRATING HAMMER, ANVIL AND STIRRUP

SENSE OF BALANCE CANALS

MEMBRANE

NERVES TO BRAIN

AUDITORY CANAL

EAR DRUM

MIDDLE EAR

BLUE AREA INDICATES FLUID FILLED INNER EAR

SOUND WAVES WHICH MAKE THE EAR-DRUM VIBRATE

Your Nose

Your nose is joined to your forehead by bone at the top, but its shape is formed by gristle, and the sides by skin and fatty tissue. The openings of the nostrils are protected by hairs, which filter the air you breathe and keep out dust. The nose has two purposes, to breathe and to smell.

The organ of smelling is called the *olfactory* system, and is situated in the upper part of the nostrils and on the partition between them, where very delicate nerve-ends connect directly to the brain.

In ordinary breathing the air passes into the nose and into the nasal canal without reaching the olfactory nerves. If you want to detect a smell you draw the air further up the nostrils by sniffing.

When air comes into contact with the olfactory nerves, messages are sent to the brain, and you smell and identify the odour. Smelling food helps you to taste it, a good plate of hot food smells good and helps the digestive processes in the mouth.

Other nerves in the lower part of the nose act as a warning system, when they are irritated you sneeze and reject anything the nose doesn't like.

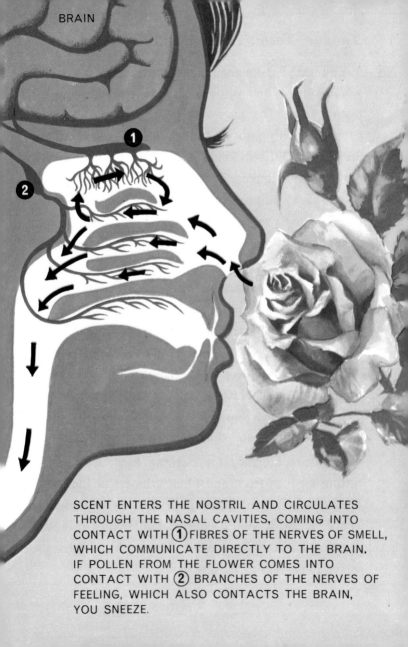

BRAIN

SCENT ENTERS THE NOSTRIL AND CIRCULATES
THROUGH THE NASAL CAVITIES, COMING INTO
CONTACT WITH (1) FIBRES OF THE NERVES OF SMELL,
WHICH COMMUNICATE DIRECTLY TO THE BRAIN.
IF POLLEN FROM THE FLOWER COMES INTO
CONTACT WITH (2) BRANCHES OF THE NERVES OF
FEELING, WHICH ALSO CONTACTS THE BRAIN,
YOU SNEEZE.

Tongue, Taste, Teeth and Talking

You use your tongue for mixing up food with saliva when you eat, and you also use it for talking and for tasting food. The *taste-buds* on the tongue's surface connect directly with your brain, and tell you what you are tasting. Different kinds of taste buds are on different parts of your tongue, as the diagram shows. You can prove this by putting sugar, salt and lemon on different parts of your own tongue.

Your tongue controls the sounds you make when you talk or sing. The sounds themselves come from your voice-box, or larynx, which is in your throat above your wind-pipe, and contains two *vocal cords*. These are normally slack to let air pass freely between them when you breathe. When you speak they are stretched tight and the air passing makes them vibrate rapidly and produce sound. The larynx has a lid, called the *epiglottis*, which closes when you swallow, to prevent food going into the windpipe and choking you.

Teeth are designed for chewing food, with sharp cutting teeth in front and blunt grinders at the back. The inside of a tooth is soft pulp which is covered with a hard, yellowish-white *dentine*, and this in turn has a thin layer of hard, white enamel. The teeth are strongly rooted in cavities in the jaw bones.

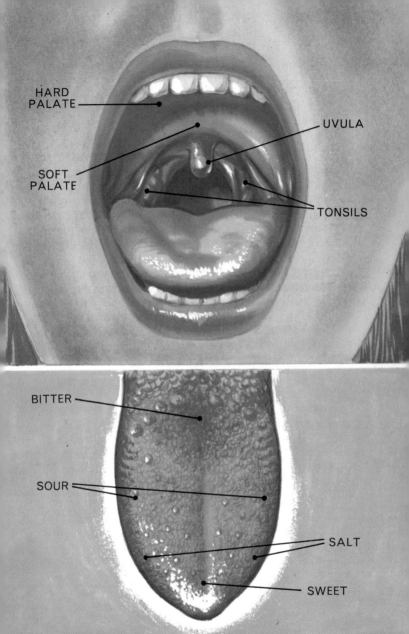

HARD PALATE

UVULA

SOFT PALATE

TONSILS

BITTER

SOUR

SALT

SWEET

How Life begins

It is from one single cell that a new life is created. This is a cell, called an ovum or egg, produced in one of the two ovaries of a female approximately every twenty-eight days, beginning at about the age of thirteen. This passes down one of the egg tubes.

Also at about the same age, the testes of the male, situated in the scrotum between the legs, are able to produce millions of sperm cells which can pass along the sperm tubes and out through the penis. When a man and woman marry and wish to have a child, the male penis is inserted inside the female vagina and the sperm cells pass in and swim towards the ovaries. If a sperm cell meets an ovum, it may fertilize the ovum and a wonderful process begins. The fertilized egg-cell attaches itself to the lining of the womb, or uterus, and begins to grow. This single cell splits to form two cells, continuing this process until thousands of cells form into a ball-like shape. Gradually these cells form a new being, an *embryo*, about a quarter of an inch long. The embryo has a head, a body (with tail at first) and a heart which circulates blood. It then develops limbs, brain, a nervous system and all the complicated organs of the body.

The embryo is protected inside the mother's womb where it is supplied with oxygen and nourishment in the mother's blood by way of a tube called the *umbilical cord*. After nine months, the fully grown baby is expelled from the womb through the vagina, by muscular contractions. The umbilical cord is then cut and the baby becomes a separate individual.

If the female egg cell is not fertilized, it is passed from the womb through the vagina, together with the lining which has previously broken down to enable it to pass away in the form of blood. This happens about every twenty-eight days and is known as *menstruation*. The lining is then renewed.

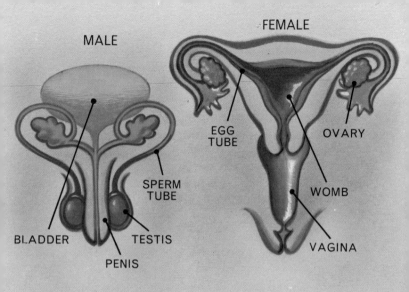

MALE

FEMALE

EGG TUBE

OVARY

SPERM TUBE

WOMB

BLADDER

TESTIS

PENIS

VAGINA

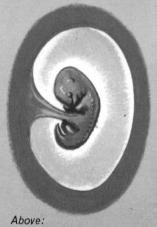

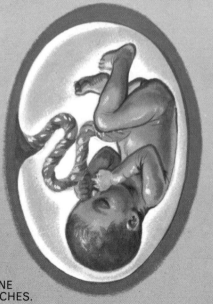

Above:

EMBRYO AT ONE MONTH. ¼ INCH LONG.

Right:

FOETUS AT NINE MONTHS. 20 INCHES.

Growing

The average length of a new-born baby is twenty inches, and the average weight about seven pounds. He has a great deal of growing to do, and a great deal to learn, before he can look after himself. Although he has not been taught anything, he does possess a certain amount of instinctive knowledge. He can breathe, feed and to a certain degree he can protect himself. If he is put down on his face he will turn his head so that he can breathe. His fingers have a remarkably strong grip, to hold on.

A baby's head is a quarter the size of his whole body, and his arms and legs are very short; his shape alters as he grows. His bones are soft and rubbery and he has no teeth.

Gradually he learns. He discovers how to focus his eyes to see, and as his limbs grow and his muscles harden he learns to sit up, then to crawl and finally to walk. Between six and nine months he begins to grow teeth.

As his brain develops he begins to remember things and to recognise people. He learns to make sounds and then to speak, first a few words at a time, and then sentences. As he grows his shape changes, his character and personality develop and the baby becomes a young child and develops into a social being.

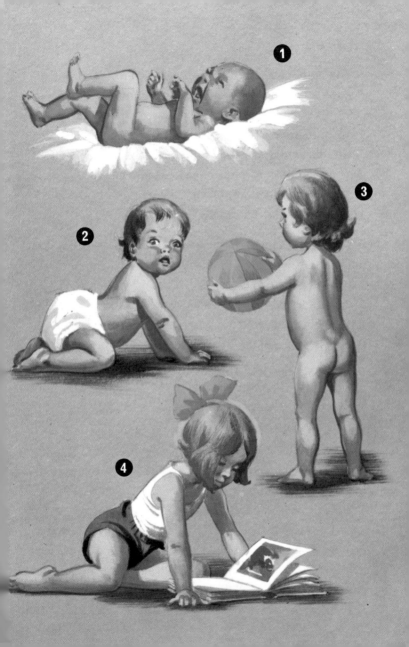

Growing up

The body helps in the process of growing up in many ways. Young bones are softer than an adult's, and more elastic. The bone-ends are covered with cartilage to make growth possible. Young eyes and ears are sharper than an adult's, and the brain is more receptive and readier to learn. A child needs a lot of exercise, and has the instinct to run about, to develop growing muscles and limbs. The skin is softer and more flexible.

The first change is the growth of second teeth to replace the first, or 'milk teeth'. Between the ages of six and thirteen, the first set of twenty is replaced by twenty-eight new ones, which may eventually become thirty-two if the four 'wisdom teeth' grow ten years later.

At about fourteen the body changes in many ways. This important stage is called *puberty*, and is followed by *adolescence*. In puberty a boy's voice 'breaks' as his vocal cords lengthen and hair begins to grow on his chin and body. Growth is rapid and the shape of the body changes, and in girls the breasts develop and menstruation, often called the 'period', begins. This is explained on the page "How Life Begins". Gradually limbs and organs become fully developed until the long process of growing up ends, and the person who was a helpless baby has become an adult man or woman.

But it hurts!

A hurt is a warning and without the ability to feel pain you would soon be in serious trouble. You could injure your hand seriously if you continued to hold something very hot, but pain-nerves flash an urgent warning and you drop it before much harm can be done. Your body cells could perish of starvation if hunger-pains did not tell you to stoke up with food. When you feel tired your body is telling you it needs rest.

Your body can mend itself. When you sleep it builds up fresh energy and brain and senses are restored to full efficiency. Some injuries can be completely repaired by the body, the most colourful ‘ black eye ’ becomes normal, a cut heals over.

If harmful bacteria get into your flesh through a cut it will ‘ fester ’, and a creamy liquid called *pus* will form. This is the white blood corpuscles which hurried to the injury and have been ‘ killed in action ’ fighting the harmful bacteria. If an infection is present, the body produces many extra white corpuscles to fight the germs.

Very often a doctor only uses his skill and knowledge to help your body to cure itself.

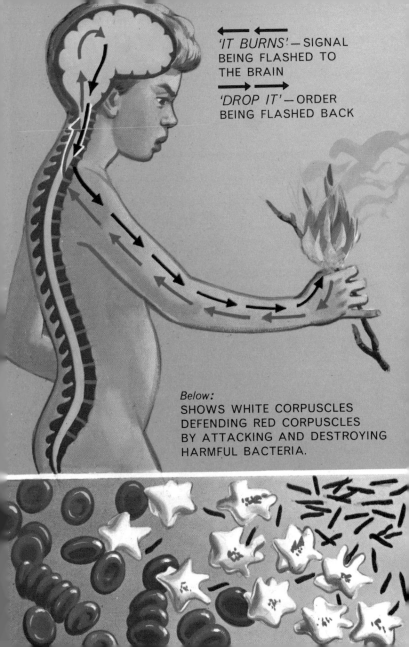

'IT BURNS' — SIGNAL BEING FLASHED TO THE BRAIN

'DROP IT' — ORDER BEING FLASHED BACK

Below:
SHOWS WHITE CORPUSCLES DEFENDING RED CORPUSCLES BY ATTACKING AND DESTROYING HARMFUL BACTERIA.

Good Health!

Your body is a highly efficient machine, wonderfully packed inside your skin, and good health is natural and normal. But you can help by being sensible.

People differ in the amount of sleep they need but a general rule is that at six years old you need twelve hours sleep; at ten, ten hours; at fourteen, nine-and-a-half and at seventeen and older, eight hours. Go to bed before you are 'tired out', and if you find it difficult to wake up you need more sleep.

Proper food is vital, as correct fuel is to an engine. Remember that fresh fruit, fresh vegetables and milk are good for you. If you *must* eat between meals have fruit or nuts, sweets can ruin your teeth.

Regular exercise is necessary, especially when you are growing. Muscles need it; it makes your blood flow faster and the deep breathing is good for your lungs. The rules of health are simple; clear the bowels every day at the same time; wash well, clean teeth, nails and hair. Work hard, play hard and be sensible about the rules of health, don't be silly enough to smoke and your body will give you the greatest blessing of all—good health!

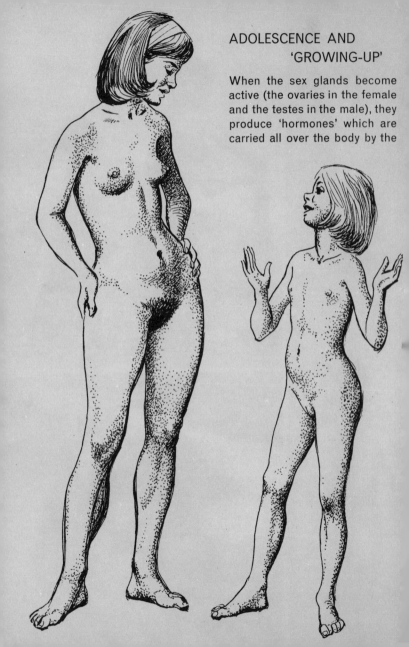

ADOLESCENCE AND 'GROWING-UP'

When the sex glands become active (the ovaries in the female and the testes in the male), they produce 'hormones' which are carried all over the body by the